Shores Of Eternity

Where Love Meets Infinity

Dushyant kumar siyag

India | USA | UK

Made with ❤ on the BookLeaf Publishing Platform
www.bookleafpub.in
www.bookleafpub.com

Dedication

To the love of my eternity

In the vast expanse of the universe, there is only one shore where my heart finds solace - the shore of your love. Every wave of longing, every tide of tears, every whisper of my soul has been drawn to the infinite beauty of your heart.

This book is a testament to the love that has consumed me, body and soul. It is a collection of whispers, screams, and prayers that have poured out of my heart in your name.

May these poems be the echoes of my love that forever resonate in the shores of your eternity.

Yours eternally
Dushyant kumar siyag

Preface

In the depths of my soul, there is a universe that exists solely for her. A universe where stars are born from the sparks of her eyes, where galaxies collide in the whispers of her name, and where time stands still in the infinite beauty of her love.

This book is a cartography of that universe, a mapping of the uncharted territories of my heart. It is a collection of poems that have been my companions on this journey of love, my confidants in the darkest hours of longing, and my celebrants in the moments of tender joy.

These poems are not just words on paper; they are the echoes of my soul, the whispers of my heart, and the screams of my love. They are the fragments of a dream that I have been chasing, the shards of a mirror that reflect the beauty of her love.

As you embark on this journey with me, I invite you to step into the shores of eternity, where love knows no bounds, and the universe is the canvas of our hearts.

May our love be the infinite ocean that we dive into, together.

Acknowledgements

This book would not have been possible without the love, support, and inspiration of those who have touched my life.

First and foremost, to the love of my eternity, who has been the celestial muse of my soul, the guiding star of my heart, and the infinite ocean of my love. Your beauty, your kindness, and your love have been the driving force behind every word, every line, and every poem in this book.

To my family, who have been my rock, my shelter, and my safe haven. Your unwavering support, your unconditional love, and your unrelenting encouragement have meant the world to me.

To my friends, who have been my fellow travelers on this journey of life. Your camaraderie, your laughter, and your tears have enriched my experiences, broadened my perspectives, and deepened my understanding of the human heart.

And to the universe, which has been my canvas, my paintbrush, and my palette. Your infinite beauty, your boundless mystery, and your eternal wonder have inspired me to create, to dream, and to love.

Thank you all for being part of this journey. May our love, our light, and our laughter illuminate the shores of eternity.

1. Love's Canvas

In the tapestry of life, a thread of gold,
Weaves a narrative of love, yet untold.
A story of laughter, of tears of joy,
A heart that overflows, like a sweet employ.

The smile that spreads, like sunrise in the sky,
Illuminates the soul, and makes the heart fly.
The eyes that sparkle, like stars on a clear night,
Reflect the beauty of love, in all its delight.

The touch that ignites, like a flame that burns bright,
Melts the fears, and soothes the soul's dark night.
The whispers that calm, like a gentle summer breeze,
Soothe the heart's deep longings, and bring it to its
knees.

Oh, love, you are the masterpiece, the work of art,
The symphony that plays, within the heart.
You are the missing piece, the one that makes us whole,
The safe haven where we find, our hearts' true goal.

2. Echoes Of You

In every crowd, I'll find a stage
To speak of you, to turn the page
Of every poem, every verse, every line
Written in the ink of love's sweet wine

I'll share with strangers, with friends and foes
The beauty of your soul, the love that glows
In every word, in every rhyme and meter
I'll echo your name, like a sweet, sweet surrender

But why, oh why, does my heart skip a beat
Whenever I think of speaking to you, my sweet retreat?
Is it the thrill of love, the rush of desire?
Or the fear of vulnerability, like a burning fire?

Perhaps it's the knowledge that my words are true
A reflection of the love I feel, pure and anew
For in your eyes, my heart finds a home
A place where love resides, and never will roam

So let me speak, let me share and proclaim
The love I feel for you, in every poem, every verse, every
name
For in the echoes of you, my heart finds its voice
A love song that whispers, a soul that makes some noise.

3. Language Of The Heart

You brought me sunshine on a rainy day,
Laughter that echoed, and chased the pain away.
You spoke a language that my heart could hear,
A poetry that touched my soul, and wiped away my
tears.

You are a verse I long to understand,
A chapter in the book of life, that I hold in my hand.
I yearn to be fluent in the language of your eyes,
To read the lines of your heart, and never say goodbye.

You are a novel that I'm still learning to read,
A story that unfolds with every kiss, every touch, every
need.
I'm drawn to the beauty of your words, the rhythm of
your soul,
A language that speaks directly to my heart, making me
whole.

Oh, to be fluent in the language of your love,

To speak the poetry of your heart, sent from above.
To read the lines of your soul, and understand the depth,
Of the love we share, the love that's meant to be our
truth.

Until then, I'll listen to the rhythm of your heart,
And learn to speak the language of our love, a work of
art.

4. Chakor's Serenade

You are the moon that I desire.
A glowing crescent in my heart's dark fire.
Or I am that Chakor, that is very far from you.
A bird that yearns to fly, yet stays with love anew.

In the stillness of the night, I feel your gentle light.
A beacon that guides me through life's plodding flight.
My heart beats fast, my soul feels alive.
When I think of you, my love and the moment.

When I meet you, I will tell you everything.
That's hidden deep within my heart, and makes me sing.
The joys, the fears, the dreams, the tears.
I'll share them all with you, through all the coming years.

I wish that time comes soon, before this age passes away.
Before the moon's pale light fades, and our love's in
disarray.
I long to be with you, to hold you close and tight.
To feel your love, your warmth, and bask in your delight.

So let us cherish every moment we share.
And make our love shine bright, like the moon in the
midnight air.
For you are the moon that I desire.
And I am the Chakor, that loves
you with heart on fire.

5. Lunar Longing

You're the moon that's closest to my heart,
Endless love for you, yet we're worlds apart.
My heart beats for you with every single word,
But alas you're distant my love, unheard.

You're the moon that's dear to every heartbeat,
My life's meaning is found in your gentle smile so sweet.
What can I say to this moonlit night so bright?
My every moment's spent in the radiance of your light.

Every whisper of my heart has been silenced without
you,
Every day feels empty, hollow and blue.
In this starry night, amidst thousands of twinkling lights,
Every unspoken heartbeat of mine is filled with your
delight.

What can I say to these countless stars up high?
My beloved, is the moon that catches my eye.
I calm these heartbeats, and whisper low and sweet,

My beloved is still far, yet forever unique.

9

6. A Heart Unseen

In the darkness, I'm lost and alone.
A heart that's been shattered, a soul that's been thrown.
Desired but never loved, a fleeting thought.
A moment's pleasure, a lifetime's fault.

I'm the ghost of what could've been.
A whispered promise, a forgotten dream.
The maybe, the what-if, the could-have-been.
A perpetual ache, a heart that's unseen.

Tears fall like autumn rain.
As I mourn the love that I'll never obtain.
A grief so profound, it echoes through my mind.
A bittersweet reminder, of what I've left behind.

In the silence, I hear the whispers of my heart.
A lonely echo, that never departs.
A reminder of the love, that I've never known.
A longing so intense, it's become my own.

I'm searching for solace, a refuge from the pain.
A place to hide, where love will never stain.
But like a mirage, it vanishes in thin air.
Leaving me with nothing, but this hollow gnawing care.

7. The Poem Of You

In every part of you, I see a poem of mine,
A masterpiece of beauty, a work of art divine.
Your eyes, like the ocean, deep and blue,
A reflection of the sky, a sight anew.

Your lips, like roses, soft and fine,
A gentle touch, a sweet decline.
Your skin, like silk, smooth and bright,
A canvas of perfection, a delight.

Your hair, like gold, a treasure to behold,
A cascade of splendor, a story to be told.
Your voice, like music, a symphony of love,
A melody that fills my heart above.

Meeting you is my wish, my heart's desire,
A dream come true, a burning fire.
But fate has other plans, it seems,
A path that's winding, a journey of dreams.

Not being able to meet you is my fate,
A bittersweet reality, a heavy weight.
Yet in my dreams, we dance and sing,
A love that's pure, a heart that clings.

So I'll hold on to these dreams,
And cherish every moment, it seems.
For every part of you has become a poem of mine,
A masterpiece of love, a work of art divine.

8. Your Eyes My Muse

Whenever I look at you my heart sings a tune.
My every word becomes poetry it's no boon.
Whatever I wanted to say to you my words take flight.
In the form of rhymes and verse it's a delight.

Your eyes they sparkle like diamonds in the sun.
My every thought it becomes a poem it's begun.
Your eyes it sets my soul aflame.
My every word it's a work of heart it's not lame.

Your eyes like stars shine bright and true.
My words like bees buzz with love anew.
Your smile like sunshine lights up my world.
My heart like a poet finds its way.

Your eyes are like the stars shining bright and true.
My love for you forever pure and new.
Your smile a ray of sunshine lights up my world.
Every word becomes poetry in every way.

So let me look in your eyes all day.
My every word it's a poem, it's play.
For whenever I look at you my heart sings.
My every word it's a work of heart it's wings.

9. A Symphony Of Love

Oh, the beauty of your eyes, like the stars in the night
A celestial wonder, a shining light
Every glance, a poem of love and grace
A reflection of the heart's sweet embrace

Your lips, a rose petal's gentle touch
A whisper of sweet nothings, a lover's hush
Every word, a poem of passion and fire
A burning desire, a love that never tires

Your skin, a canvas of art divine
A masterpiece of beauty, a treasure so fine
Every brush stroke, a poem of love and grace
A testament to the heart's sweet embrace

Your touch, a symphony of delight
A melody of love, a poem so bright
Every caress, a poem of joy and bliss
A celebration of love, a heavenly kiss

Your laughter, a chorus of pure delight
A poem of joy, a symphony so bright
Every note, a testament to love's pure light
A celebration of life, a sweet, sweet sight

Oh, the beauty of every part of you
A poem of love, a work of art so true
Meeting you is my wish, not being able to meet you is
my fate
But in my dreams, our love will forever create.

10. Stellar Love

Oh, the stars in the sky, so bright and so high.
A celestial ballet, a wondrous sight.
You are my love, the one I can never get.
But your presence brings me peace, a blessed bet.

With every twinkle of light, my heart feels a lift.
A warmth that spreads and a sense of right.
In your love, my soul finds a home to shift.
A place to rest, a place to be, a place to lift.

The world may be vast, the universe grand.
But you, my love make my heart understand.
The beauty of life, the joy it can hand.
A love so true, a love so grand.

So let the stars shine bright,
and let the night be peaceful.
For in my heart, you are my love eternally.

11. Tears From The Sky

In the morning light I spoke to the sky so blue.
Of the love I hold dear and the ache I feel anew.
I told the clouds of my longing and the wind did sigh.
As the raindrops fell like tears to the ground so dry.

The sky it listened well and it wept with me.
As the rain poured down a symphony.
The drops they whispered sweet nothings in my ear.
Of the love we shared and the memories so clear.

The world it was wet but my heart felt dry.
For in the rain I found a solace a sigh.
The sky it understood and it brought me peace.
As the rain it cease and the sun did release.

The sky it rained for me and it soothed my soul.
For in its tears I found a goal.
To hold on to love no matter the cost.
For in the rain I found a loss.

12. Beyond The Stars

Oh, the stars in the sky, they twinkle and shine,
A celestial display, so fine and so divine.
But my love, you are far beyond their reach,
A treasure so precious, a heart so meek.

Your eyes, they sparkle like diamonds so bright,
A gem that outshines all the stars in sight.
Your touch, it sets my soul aflame,
A passion so pure, a love so tame.

Though I may never hold you in my arms,
Your memory brings me peace, a solace that charms.
For in the night, when the stars align,
I find solace in your love, so divine.

Oh, the stars may be out of my reach,
But your love, it shines so bright, a beacon to teach.
That true love knows no bounds, no distance, no space,
A love that gives me peace, a love that finds its place.

13. Life's Symphony

Life's piano plays a tender tune,
Black keys whisper sorrow's poignant refrain soon,
White keys dance with joy's radiant light,
Together weaving a harmonious sight.

Darkness lends depth to the melody's sway,
Light illuminates the path to a brighter day,
Every key has its purpose, its role to play,
In life's grand symphony, each note sways.

Shadows of pain shape resilience's might,
Brilliance of joy kindles hope's warm light,
Imperfect, yet sublime; fragile, yet bold,
Life's masterpiece echoes the human heart's unfold.

In harmony, contrasts blend and meet,
Joy and sorrow, darkness and light retreat,
Every moment, every note, contributes to the whole,
Life's grand symphony, a majestic soul.

14. Entwined Hearts

In twists of fate, we find ourselves astray.
Lost in thought, with no direction to sway.
But then we meet, and the world slows down.
As if time itself has stopped, and all is found.

Their smile, a ray of sunshine so bright.
Lights up the path, banishing the night.
With every step, our hearts entwine.
As if we've known each other for a divine.

Their laughter echoes through our minds.
A melody that never leaves our kind.
We find solace in their eyes.
A warmth that dries our tears, and never dies.

In their embrace, we find our home.
A place where we can be ourselves, and roam.
With them by our side, life is a breeze.
A feeling that we never have to cease.

Cherish this bond we share.
This connection that's beyond compare.
For in their presence, we find our peace.
A feeling that we never have to release.

15. Forever In My Dreams

In the realm of dreams, I still behold your face,
A vision of perfection, in a secret place.
Time and distance, they cannot erase,
The love we shared, the memories we've made.

Like a beacon in the night, your love shines bright,
A guiding light that navigates the darkest of plights.
In the silence, I hear your whisper, soft and low,
A gentle reminder of the love that we've known.

Though we may be apart, in body and in space,
In my dreams, we're together, in a love that time won't
erase.
A memory that's forever etched, a love that's pure and
true,
A bond that transcends the boundaries of me and you.

So let the dreams continue, let the visions unfold,
For in their beauty, our love will never grow old.
And though we may be apart, in this life we lead,

In eternity, our love will forever be the thread.

That weaves our hearts together, a tapestry so fine,
A love that's timeless, ageless, and forever divine.
So I'll hold on to these dreams, these visions of our love,
And cherish every moment, sent from above.

16. Beauty Like Nature

You are the moon that glows with gentle light,
A beacon in the darkness, a guiding sight.
Your eyes are stars that twinkle like diamonds bright,
Reflecting the beauty that shines with inner light.

Your hair is like the wind that whispers through the
trees,
A soft and soothing melody that brings me to my knees.
It dances in the breeze with a gentle, carefree sway,
A mesmerizing sight that takes my breath away.

Your smile is like the sunrise, a warm and golden glow,
A new beginning every time, a love that forever grows.
It lights the world with radiance, a beauty to behold,
A treasure to cherish, a love that never grows old.

Your laughter is like birds chirping in the morning dew,
A joyful sound that fills my heart with love anew.
It's music to my ears, a symphony so sweet,
A treasure to behold, a love that can't be beat.

You are a beauty like nature, wild and free,
A treasure to cherish, a love that's meant to be.
You are the sunshine in my day, the stars that light my
night,
A love that shines so bright, a beauty that's pure delight.

Forever with you is where I want to be,
A love so strong and free, wild and carefree.
You are the moon, the stars, the wind, the sunrise high,
A love that I adore, a beauty that touches the sky.

17. Secret Love

I've lost so many dear ones along the way,
Some to death, some to distance, day by day.
My heart has been broken, shattered and worn,
But then I met you, and my heart was reborn.

I dare not speak my love, for fear of being apart,
I know our worlds are different, a gap that's hard to start.
But in my silence, I'll hold you dear,
A secret love, a hidden tear.

Your smile is enough, a radiant light,
Your twinkling eyes, a guiding sight.
I wish you all the happiness, a life so free,
Though I may not be with you, my heart will always be.

If ever I hear you're crying, my eyes will flow with tears,
For in your pain, my heart will ache through the years.
Though we may never meet, though our love may never
be,
In my heart, you'll always be, a love that's meant to be.

18. Love That Shines

Oh, my moon, a glowing orb of light,
Reflecting the love that shines so bright.
Give her my love, a gentle, tender breeze,
That whispers sweet nothings, and brings her to her
knees.

Give her my smile, a radiant beam of delight,
That illuminates her world, and makes her heart take
flight.
Make her eyes shine, like stars on a clear, dark night,
Reflecting the love that we share, a love that's strong and
bright.

I showed you my heart, a vulnerable, open door,
And you received it with love, and forever changed me
more.
You are like a gazing light, in the darkest of the ocean
deep,
A guiding star that shines so bright, and helps me
navigate my soul's dark keep.

In the darkest of nights, when fears and doubts assail,
Your love is a beacon of hope, that shines like a radiant
sail.
You are my safe haven, my peaceful, quiet shore,
Where I can be myself, and forever adore.

Oh, my moon, you are a treasure, a precious, shining
light,
That illuminates my world, and makes my heart sing
with delight.
Forever and always, my love for you will shine,
A constant, guiding star, that navigates my heart's dark
mine.

19. Eyes Of Truth

When I see into your eyes,
A sensation runs through my mind,
A feeling that it's going to hurt,
If you leave without being kind.

Your eyes are like a window to my soul,
A reflection of my heart's control,
I see the depths of your emotion,
And the pain that we've known.

If you leave without listening,
The hurt will linger and keep glistening,
A wound that will never heal,
A memory that will never fade.

But if you stay and listen to me,
The hurt will slowly dissipate,
And though it may still hurt to see,
Our love will find its way to be.

So look into my eyes, my dear,
And see the truth that's here,
For in your eyes, I see my fate,
And the love that will never abate.

20. In Its Own Sweet Time

In twilight's hush where shadows dance and play.
Everything waits for its time, they say.
A rosebud swollen with promise pauses in its sway.
For only when the time is right, it'll bloom and sway.

The sun a fiery orb suspended in the sky.
Awaiting its cue before it doth arise high.
And though we may impatiently pace and fret.
The universe moves at its own divine beat.

So wait dear heart for yours is on its way.
One who belongs to you will come to stay.
In time they'll arrive and your heart will sing.
For love like the sun blooms in its own sweet time.

21. Unspoken Words

Every day I think of you, my heart longs to speak,
But every day I miss you, and my words cannot seek,
The depths of my feelings, the pain they do bring,
Every day I want to talk to you, but my heart won't sing.

The memories we made, the laughter we shared,
The moments we spent, the love we bared,
I miss it all, I miss you so,
Every day I think of you, my heart does glow.

But my heart don't want to bother you,
It knows that you have your own life to pursue,
I don't want to be a burden, I don't want to be a pest,
Every day I think of you, and my heart is at rest.

So I'll hold my words, and keep them inside,
And hope that someday, you'll be my side,
And we'll be together, where we once did stride,
Every day I think of you, my heart does reside.

22. Boundless Love

In the echoes of my hollowed heart,
where shadows of loved ones depart,
I find myself lost, yet again.
Some fled with fate's cruel hand,
while others vanished like grains of sand.

But then, I see you, and my soul revives.
Though our worlds may be apart,
in status and in life, your smile is my solace,
my guiding light.

Your twinkling eyes, like stars in the night,
illuminate the darkness, make my heart take flight.
I wish you all the joy, all the love,
all the happiness that life can bring.

If ever tears should fall from your eyes,
mine would flow like rivers, a deluge of sorrow,
a heart that beats for you alone.

23. Healing Heart

You were the spark that lit my way,
A love that taught me to live each day.
In a world that had left me broken and worn,
You showed me how to heal, how to be reborn.

Maybe I had lost the feeling, the spark,
The joy of being alive, of leaving my mark.
But then I met you, and my heart revived,
The joy of having a good time, of feeling alive.

You are the sunshine that brightens my day,
The calm in every storm, the safe haven where I can stay.
You are the love that heals my soul,
The missing piece that makes me whole.

24. Soulful Solace

In the silence of my soul, I hear your voice,
A whispered promise, a heartfelt choice.
In the stillness of the night, I feel your presence near,
A gentle breeze that soothes my fear.

In the quiet moments, I reflect on our past,
The memories we've shared, the love that will forever
last.
In the silence of my soul, I find my peace,
A sense of calm that only love can release.

25. Forever Heart

In the depths of my heart, there's a place for you,
A space that's reserved, forever true.
Where memories of our love will forever stay,
And in my dreams, I'll see your face each day.

Time may pass, and seasons may change,
But in my heart, our love will forever range.
Through every moment, every breath I take,
You'll be with me, forever in my heart, for our love's
sake.

26. Eternal Flame

In the velvety blackness of night's dark shroud,
A radiant flame flickers, a love beacon avowed.
Through tempests' wild turmoil, through time's relentless
sway,
Our love remains, an unwavering, eternal refrain.

Like a rose in full bloom, its petals unfurled in delight,
Our love will flourish, nourished by tears, laughter, and
love's warm light.
In every fleeting moment, with every breath I draw,
Our love will burn, an eternal, fiery passion, that will
never dwindle or wane.

27. Celestial Love

She is the moon's silken glow,
A soft luminescence that dissolves the night's dark woe.
Her eyes, like diamonds in the celestial sea,
Shine bright and true, a guiding light that navigates me.

Her voice is a zephyr's gentle sigh,
A whispered promise that soothes my soul's dark sky.
In her presence, I am wrapped in peaceful calm,
A sense of serenity that only she can balm.

She is my heart's north star, my guiding light,
The one who illuminates my world, banishing the dark
of night.
In her love, I find my haven, my peaceful nest,
A sense of belonging that I've never known, and love the
best.

28. A Secret Adoration

In secret, I behold her radiant form,
A vision of beauty that my heart cannot transform.
Her eyes, like sapphires shining bright and blue,
Would see the depths of my soul, and all my secrets
anew.

I know she dwells in a world apart,
Where I am but a whispered rumor, a distant, fading
heart.
Yet still, I'm grateful for the fleeting glimpse,
Of her living life to the fullest, with joy that dances and
prances.

Though I may not be a thread in the tapestry of her days,
I'm consoled by the knowledge that she's living life in
vibrant hues and rays.
Her laughter echoes, a melodic refrain,
A bittersweet reminder of the love that remains in vain.

29. Legacy Of Love

In whispers of the past, I hear your name,
A gentle breeze that stirs the flames,
Of memories we forged, in laughter and in tears,
A legacy of love, that lasts for years.

Like autumn leaves, our moments fell,
A colorful tapestry, that time will tell,
Each thread a story, of joy and of strife,
A testament to love, that cuts through life.

In forgotten scents, I smell your perfume,
A fragrance that transports, to a bygone room,
Where love and laughter, once filled the air,
And memories were made, without a single care.

Though time may take, our bodies away,
Our memories remain, to light the way,
For those who come, after we are gone,
A legacy of love, that will live on.

30. A Love In Ink

In every line, in every rhyme,
You are the muse, the heart's sweet crime.
My words are whispers, a love so true,
A symphony of emotions, all because of you.

You live in my poems, a gentle breeze,
A soothing melody that brings me to my knees.
In every verse, I pour my heart and soul,
A love letter to you, a work of art, a legacy whole.

You are the meaning of love, the essence of my heart,
The reason I write, the reason I never depart.
Though we may never meet, though our love may
remain unseen,
It lives in my words, a silent love, a love serene.

I am happy in this love, a love that's pure and true,
A love that transcends time and space, a love that shines
through.
In every poem, in every line,

You are the love that makes my heart entwine.

31. The End

45

Thank you for being a part of my poetic journey. What do you think is the most powerful way to express love? Write and tag me on Instagram @dushyantsiyag

9 789369 539130